Bath & Kitchen

HINTS & TIPS

Publications International, Ltd.

Fuller Brush logo and images © 2017 Fuller Brush.
www.fuller.com

Cover and interior art: Fuller Brush, Getty, Shutterstock.com

This publication © 2017 Publications International, Ltd. All rights reserved. This publication may not be reproduced or quoted in whole or in part by any means whatsoever without written permission from Publications International, Ltd. Permission is never granted for commercial purposes.

Louis Weber, CEO
Publications International, Ltd.
8140 Lehigh Avenue
Morton Grove, IL 60053

Permission is never granted for commercial purposes.

ISBN: 978-1-68022-797-0

Manufactured in China.

8 7 6 5 4 3 2 1

CONTENTS

In The Kitchen

- **6** Keep Your Kitchen Clutter-Free
- **8** Kitchen Knives and Cutting Boards
- **10** Baking Sheets and Non-Stick Cookware
- **11** Food Storage
- **12** Food Preparation Hacks
- **14** Prevent Mess While You Cook
- **17** Smell-Busters
- **19** Sinks and Fixtures
- **20** Drains
- **21** Garbage Disposals
- **22** Fridge and Freezer
- **24** Cleaning Countertops
- **25** Oven and Stovetop
- **27** Microwave
- **28** Coffee and Teapots
- **29** Dishwasher
- **30** Containers
- **31** Dinnerware and Glassware
- **34** Flatware and Cutlery
- **36** Pots and Pans: Basic Care
- **38** Burned-on Food and Grease
- **39** Prevent and Remove Rust
- **40** Stains and Discoloration
- **41** Cast-Iron Care
- **42** Copper Care
- **43** Non-Stick Cookware
- **44** Small Appliances

CONTENTS
In The Bathroom

- **46** Daily Cleaning Tips
- **48** Countertops
- **51** Showers and Bathtubs
- **53** Sinks
- **54** Mildew Fighters
- **55** Grout
- **56** Smell-Busters
- **57** Toilets
- **60** Drains
- **62** Mirrors
- **63** Solving Bathroom Clutter
- **64** A Few Last Tips

Introduction

In 1906, Alfred Fuller founded the company that became the Fuller Brush company. For decades, the company has been providing household products and cleaning supplies to make maintaining a household easier. In this book, you'll find some advice and strategies that focus on your kitchen and bathroom.

Let's start off in the kitchen. Like all of us, you probably want a clean kitchen. You want shiny pots and pans, a stovetop free of caked on food, and clear glassware. It's a little easier said than done, but it is doable. Cooking is a messy task, but if you clean as you go and do a quick clean at the end of the day, you'll be well on your way!

Keep Your Kitchen Clutter-Free

Our kitchens can become cluttered over time, leaving you to find yourself rummaging through drawers to find serving spoons and having to discard a pile of mail to see the top of the kitchen table. Here are some tips to help.

• Drawers getting cluttered with one-use gadgets? Once a year, go through and discard gadgets you haven't used in the last year. Don't just think of whether you might use them—base your decision on whether you have in recent memory.

When you're doing that, think about what items you use most frequently. Place those utensils, pots, and pans in easy-to-reach locations.

Keep Your Kitchen Clutter Free • 7

• Buy a drawer organizer to keep your cutlery neat and tidy, so you're not rummaging through a drawer with open knives.

• Save space and keep place mats handy by hanging them inside a pantry or cabinet door. Clip a set together with a binder clip.

• Group cloth napkin sets together in a drawer or hall pantry with a binder clip. When it's time to set the table for company, you'll have a full set at the ready.

• Most people don't use good cloth tablecloths and napkins every night or even every week. To prevent the creases that form when linens are folded for storage, roll the linens onto cardboard tubes covered with cling wrap. Use paper towel tubes for napkins and gift wrap tubes for tablecloths.

• Keep your cookbooks away from the heat of the stove.

• Appliance cords tangling? Use Velcro to bind them together neatly.

• If you only use some appliances a few times a year, don't let them take up valuable space on the countertop. Instead, store them away.

• It's easy to collect an untidy pile of plastic food storage containers. For a few weeks, see how many plastic food storage containers you generally use—you might use far less than you think. Pack away the remainder in storage. If you haven't pulled it out of storage after a month or two, discard.

• Store the lids of plastic food storage vertically. This allows you to pull out just one of the appropriate size without having to sift through an unwieldy stack.

Kitchen Knives and Cutting Boards

There's a lot of chopping involved in cooking. Vegetables, meat, fish—your knives and cutting boards are some of the most useful items in your kitchen. Take care of them, and they'll take care of you.

- You don't need to buy an expensive knife set with a knife for every need. A simpler set with three or four knives, including a paring knife and a chef knife, will serve you well.

- Don't leave your knife in the sink—clean it immediately after use.

Cutting an onion? A sharper knife will help keep tears at bay. Other tips that might help: soak the onion in water or freeze it for 10 minutes beforehand, peel it under running water, or chew a piece of bread or gum while cutting.

Kitchen Knives and Cutting Boards • 9

• Don't clean your knives in the dishwasher—they will last longer and serve you better if you hand wash them.

• Ingredients such as dried fruits won't stick to a knife if you rub a bit of vegetable oil on the blade before chopping.

• You can keep odors from a clean wood or plastic cutting board by wiping it with a sponge dampened with a little vinegar.

• After cleaning your wood cutting board, rub a bit of lemon juice on it to help get rid of garlic, onion, or fish smells.

• Use bleach to keep a wood cutting board free of bacteria. Wash the cutting board in hot, sudsy water and rinse thoroughly. Then mix 3 tablespoons bleach with 1 gallon warm water. Soak or brush the solution onto the cutting board, keep it moist for at least 2 minutes, then rinse thoroughly.

• Deodorize and remove stains from wood cutting boards, bowls, or utensils with a solution of 4 tablespoons baking soda to 1 quart water.

• To disinfect a plastic cutting board after it's been washed, place it in a solution of 1 tablespoon bleach per gallon of water. Soak for 2 minutes; drain and air-dry.

• Plastic, non-stick cutting mats are also available on the market. If you buy an array in different colors, you can use a different color for each type of food to prevent cross-contamination.

Baking Sheets and Non-Stick Cookware

• Before you buy casserole dishes, roasting pans, and cookie sheets, check whether they're non-stick. Investing in non-stick cookware will save you a lot of cleaning time over the years!

• Keep dough from sticking to cookie cutters with a light application of cooking spray beforehand.

• Or, instead of greasing cookie sheets, line them with parchment paper. The cookies bake more evenly, they cool right on the pan, and cleanup is minimal.

• Cookies lift off a cookie sheet easily if you run a piece of unflavored dental floss underneath them.

• To grease a pan or cookie sheet with shortening, slip a food storage bag over your hand and dip it directly into the shortening container. Rub your hand over the pan to spread the shortening. Keep the bag in the shortening container for next time.

Food Storage

- Keep potatoes from sprouting by storing apples with them.

- Cut fruit will stay fresh in the refrigerator without turning brown if you coat it with lemon juice.

- Many fruits ripen more quickly and evenly at room temperature in a paper lunch bag. These include tomatoes, peaches, pears, and avocados. When the produce is sufficiently ripened, refrigerate as usual. Wrap green bananas first in a damp dishtowel, then place in bag.

- Before you stow uncut lemons in the refrigerator, put them in a jar of water. They will be juicier and will last longer than lemons stored in the produce drawer.

- Tomatoes ripen best when placed stem-side up, not touching each other, and out of direct sunlight. They may look nice on a windowsill, but that may cause soft spots.

Before we had freezers and refrigerators, salt was an important preservative and one of only a few ways to keep food from spoiling. Salt was a valuable trade commodity and could even be used as a currency, and our word "salary" comes from salt.

Food Preparation Hacks

- Picking silk from a freshly shucked ear of corn can be a tedious job. Speed up the process by wiping a damp paper towel across the ear; it will pick up the strands.

- Dry lettuce faster than you can say "spin cycle"! Wash the leaves and shake off as much water as you can. Place them in a plastic grocery bag lined with paper towels. Grasp the bag by the handles (or let your kids have the fun) and whirl it around in circles until the lettuce is dry.

- Slightly wilted produce can be brought back to life if you sprinkle it with cool water, wrap in a paper towel, and refrigerate for about an hour.

- Hard cheeses that are difficult to cut can be tamed by cutting through them with unflavored dental floss.

- Hold an orange under hot water for a bit before you squeeze it. You'll get twice the juice!

- If a lemon is too firm to juice, try either of these methods: Microwave it on high in 10-second increments until it is soft enough, or boil it for a few minutes.

- To get just a few drops of juice from a lemon or lime, pierce the whole fruit with a toothpick. Squeeze out what you need, then use the toothpick to plug the hole. Refrigerate.

Food Preparation Hacks • 13

• Salt can help remove gritty dirt from fresh vegetables. To wash arugula, leeks, or spinach, trim them and place in a bowl of lukewarm water. Add a tablespoon of salt, swish vegetables around, and let soak for 20 to 30 minutes. Transfer vegetables to a colander and rinse thoroughly.

• Keep a spray bottle of vinegar near your kitchen sink and use it to spritz vegetables before you rinse them with cold running water. The vinegar will help dissolve pesticide residue.

• Tomatoes are easier to peel if you place them in a heatproof bowl and cover them with boiling water. Wait 1 minute, then drain.

• Freshen up fish just brought home from the market by returning it to its natural environment for a short time. Add 1 tablespoon sea salt to 2 quarts cold water, then add a lot of ice cubes. Soak fish in this salt water for about 15 minutes, then remove and dry it off before preparing as desired.

• It's easiest to marinate meats not in a bowl or pan but in a quart-size or gallon-size food storage bag. The bag allows for full coverage, and you can easily flip the bag at intervals to make sure the marinade reaches all parts of the meat.

• Grind peppercorns or crush other whole spices by placing them in a snack-size food storage bag and smashing with a meat-tenderizing hammer or even a rolling pin.

Prevent Mess While You Cook

• Mix and dispense in 2 easy steps—no cleanup required! Mix ingredients for deviled eggs or stuffed mushrooms by placing all ingredients in a plastic food storage bag. Seal it and knead to blend contents. To dispense the mixture, snip off a small corner of the still-sealed bag. Then just squeeze and stuff! When you're done, throw away your "dispenser."

• When you need cracker crumbs for a recipe, put your crackers in a plastic food storage bag and squeeze out most of the air. Seal it almost all the way, leaving it open at the corner so air can escape. Crush crackers by rolling a rolling pin up and down the bag. This contains the mess, crushes the crackers, and keeps your rolling pin clean.

- Before you prepare food on a countertop, cover the surface with a large sheet of either wax or parchment paper. Put it under any cutting boards too. This is especially important when working with meat, chicken, or fish.

- Spread a sheet of aluminum foil on the oven rack below a baking pan if you fear boilovers and spills. (Don't spread the foil on the bottom of an oven.)

- Pots are less likely to boil over when you use this tiny tool: a tiny toothpick laid flat between the lid and the pot. The space allows just enough steam to escape to prevent boilovers. This works when baking covered casserole dishes too.

- Melt chocolate without the messy bowl or pan to wash afterward. Pour chocolate chips, squares, or pieces into a plastic food storage bag and squeeze out most of the air. Seal and place bag in a pan of warm (but not boiling) water. When the chocolate is melted, snip off a small corner of the still-sealed bag; squeeze it into a recipe or use it to decorate a cake.

- Keep that cookbook clean while you cook. Open it to the proper page, then cover it with or enclose it in a plastic food storage bag.

- Picking up the mess from a dropped egg can be tricky. Make it easier by sprinkling the mess with salt and letting stand 15 minutes. The salt absorbs and solidifies the runny egg. Wipe away with a paper towel.

16 • Prevent Mess While You Cook

• If you spill a small amount of cooking oil, sprinkle it with salt. Wipe up spill after about 15 minutes.

• Add a quick shot of cooking spray to the lip of a measuring cup or pitcher to prevent drips.

• Clearing the table after a big dinner party can be a challenge. To get a head start on doing the dishes, line a large bowl with a plastic grocery bag, handles overlapping the edges. Place it prominently in your kitchen with a rubber spatula alongside. As the plates are brought into the kitchen, scrape the scraps right into the bowl. Once the plates are clean, it's a snap to pick the bag up by the handles and toss.

• Save yourself some steps and keep your countertops neater. Line a coffee can with a small plastic bag; place it near the sink and fill it with peelings and scraps. Make just 1 trip to the kitchen trash to toss the bag when you're done rather than traipsing back and forth.

• When you can't wash the breakfast dishes immediately, sprinkle plates with salt to keep eggs from sticking and make dishes easier to clean later.

• Soft cheese or other sticky food stuck on a grater? Cut a lemon in half and rub the pulp side on both surfaces of the grater.

• Place an entire roll or coil of garbage bags in the bottom of your garbage can. When you fill up one bag, remove it and just pull up a new one.

• If you spill a small amount of cooking oil, sprinkle it with salt. Wipe up spill after about 15 minutes.

Smell-Busters

• Garlic and onion odors on countertops respond to a solution of 1 tablespoon bleach and 1 cup water. Wash the surface, then let the solution sit for about 5 minutes. Rinse well.

• If you come home to a foul-smelling fridge full of leftovers you forgot to trash before your trip, toss the mess immediately. Clean up any excess with a sponge or a paper towel, then gather 6 or more coffee filters. Fill each filter with 1/2 cup baking soda; place 1 or more on each shelf and compartment to absorb odors quickly. Remove when odor is gone.

• Kitchen odors disappear thanks to the freshening power of lemons and a few spices. Fill a small pot with water. Add several pieces of lemon rind and about 1 teaspoon each of whole cloves and rosemary leaves. Bring to a boil. The aroma will soon reach nearly every room of your house.

• Freshen the air in your kitchen with the simplest of methods. Heat the oven to 300 degrees Fahrenheit and place a whole lemon on the center rack. With the door slightly ajar, let the lemon "cook" for about 15 minutes; turn off oven. Let lemon cool before removing it.

• Disguise burnt smells with a touch of ground cinnamon. Sprinkle a bit in a pie plate and place in a warm oven for about 10 minutes.

18 • Smell-Busters

• Boil 1 tablespoon vinegar in 1 cup water to eliminate smoky smells in the kitchen.

• Freshen a plastic lunch box by filling it with water and 1/4 cup vinegar. Let stand for 12 hours, then rinse with fresh water. An open box of baking soda in the refrigerator or freezer absorbs odors for up to 3 months.

• Remove fish, onion, or garlic odor from hands with a solution of 3 parts baking soda to 1 part water or hand soap. Rub, then rinse.

• Alternately, rub a few coffee beans in your hands; the oil released absorbs the odor. Wash your hands with soap and warm water once the odor is gone.

• To remove onion odor from your hands, sprinkle on a little salt, then moisten with a bit of vinegar. Rub hands together and rinse.

Sinks and Fixtures

• Get in the habit of wiping faucets and taps when you swab the counters after meals. This will prevent water spots and give your kitchen a sparkling look with very little effort on your part.

• Clean hardware when you clean the sink, using the same cleaning product and method. Rinse well and buff with a dry cloth.

• If you live in an area that has hard water, you'll need to remove mineral deposits from faucet heads. Remove the head from its fitting, take it apart, and soak it in vinegar. Then brush the mineral deposits loose with a toothbrush. If the holes remain clogged, poke them clear with a wire, pin, toothpick, or ice pick.

• Just one dryer sheet can control odor and musty smells under your bathroom or kitchen sink.

Drains

We all know that cooking grease combined with bits of food jams kitchen-sink drains, and we know that prevention is the best cure for the problem. Germs thrive in sink drains. Use a brush to clean them often!

If you notice your drain running more slowly, treat it; don't wait until no water drains out. Here are some solutions.

• Pour a strong salt solution of 1 cup salt and 2 cups hot water down the kitchen drain to eliminate odors and break up grease deposits.

• To dislodge greasy foods that may be clogging up your drain, sprinkle 1/2 cup salt and 1/2 cup baking soda into the drain. Run hot tap water to flush.

• Pour 1/2 cup baking soda down the drain, followed by 1 cup distilled white vinegar. When foam subsides, rinse with hot water. This also works well on garbage disposals.

• Clear kitchen sink drainpipes of food particles that breed mold and bacteria. Once a week, pour in a solution of 1 tablespoon bleach in 1 gallon water. Wait a few minutes, then flush with cold running water for several minutes.

Garbage Disposals

Clean and freshen your garbage disposal periodically with a garbage disposal cleaner.

To remove odors from a garbage disposal, cut up a lemon, toss it in, and grind it up. Oranges and limes also work to freshen the disposal.

Fridge and Freezer

If you keep up appearances by regularly wiping sticky fingerprints off the refrigerator door and gummy drips off the front of the freezer, you can put off cleaning the messes that lurk within your large appliances until you have time to deal with them thoroughly.

Fridge and Freezer • 23

• To clean and refresh the inside of your refrigerator, sprinkle equal amounts of salt and baking soda onto a damp sponge and wipe down all surfaces. Wipe clean with a fresh sponge dampened with water.

• Remove mildew spots and prevent mildew buildup inside your refrigerator by wiping occasionally with a sponge dampened in undiluted vinegar. A toothbrush is an excellent tool for reaching inside the folds of the rubber seals. No need to rinse afterward.

• Use a clean, dry toothbrush to remove crumbs and crud from the seals around refrigerator and freezer doors.

• Place a sheet of aluminum foil on the floor of your freezer to keep spills and ice cube trays from sticking. Be sure not to cover any vents or other openings.

• Trying to vacuum under the refrigerator or another hard-to-reach spot? Put a cardboard tube from a roll of paper towels, gift wrap, or another product on the end of the hose attachment. For narrow openings, bend or flatten the tube.

• Don't waste a ruined pair of pantyhose—use it to clean under your refrigerator. Wrap the nylon around a yardstick, then run it under the fridge.

• To remove any unpleasant taste in ice cubes from an automatic ice cube maker, clean the removable parts of the unit with baking soda and water.

Cleaning Countertops

- A concentrated degreaser can be used on hard surfaces—one bottle can make lots of cleaning solution. Just add water!

- When you buy a countertop cleaner, check first what kind of surfaces it can be used for.

- For light cleaning, use club soda to clean your kitchen counters, stovetop, and stainless-steel fixtures. Just pour it directly on a sponge and wipe clean. Rinse with warm water, then dry thoroughly.

- Butcher-block and other wood countertops require more care than you might expect, if you don't want them to look like they belong in the back room of a butcher shop. Always use a cutting board on a wood countertop, just as you would with any other surface. Wipe up stains and keep your wood countertops as dry as you possibly can. Periodically, rub oil into wood countertops to protect them from moisture.

- Wipe your kitchen countertops with undiluted distilled white vinegar once a day to shine them and keep your kitchen smelling fresh.

- To get rid of odors, rub the surface with a slice of lemon.

Oven and Stovetop

Ovens and stovetops can be a hot mess. Here are a few tips to help. Stove and oven cleaners are available on the market. Always read instructions first to check if the oven needs to be warm or cool.

- Always address a stovetop spill quickly. Don't let food dry and harden.

- Stovetop spills can be cleaned up easily if first sprinkled with salt. The mildly abrasive quality of salt will remove stuck-on food, but it won't mar your stove's surface.

- Clean burned-on food from a stovetop burner by sprinkling it with a mixture of salt and ground cinnamon, then wiping away immediately. The mixture will give off a pleasant smell and cover up any burnt odor the next time you turn on the burner.

- Soak up liquid spills on stovetop burners in much the same way, sprinkling with a mixture of salt and ground cinnamon. Leave mixture on spill for 5 minutes to absorb liquid, then wipe away.

26 • Oven and Stovetop

• Combine equal parts vinegar and hot water in a small bowl. Use this solution and a sponge to rub away any dried-on stains in your oven and help prevent grease buildup.

• Eliminate the odor from a commercial oven cleaner with a solution of 2 cups vinegar and 3 quarts warm water. Dip a sponge into mixture and wring it well, then wipe down the inside surfaces of the oven. There's no need to rinse.

• If a pie or similar sugary confection boils over in your oven, sprinkle the sticky spill with salt while the oven is still hot. Let it sit until spilled area becomes crisp, then lift off with a spatula when oven cools.

• A similar technique for loosening burned-on foods from oven or grill racks is to place the racks in a trash bag. Mix 1 cup baking soda and 1/2 cup ammonia and pour over the racks. Close the bag and let sit overnight. Scrub and rinse well in the morning.

• Use a degreaser to cut grease buildup on stoves, backsplashes, or glossy enamel surfaces.

• Clean up a grease spatter on the kitchen wall with a bit of cornstarch on a paper towel or soft cloth. Gently rub the grease spot until it's gone.

• To clean a hamburger grill or pancake griddle, pour brewed coffee onto the surface (the surface can be warm or cold). Wait a few minutes, then wipe clean with a soft cloth—make sure the surface has cooled before you do this.

Microwave

• It's easy to overlook the microwave—you don't see the stains when the door is shut! But don't let stains build up—use a microwave oven cleaner periodically. You can make it part of your cleaning habit—checking the microwave every time you run the dishwasher, for example.

• Vinegar is also a great tool for microwaves. To remove the lingering smell of burned microwave popcorn, heat a small glass dish of pure vinegar in the microwave for 5 minutes on a low heat setting. Remove and wipe down inside of oven.

• Deodorize your microwave by keeping a dish of vinegar inside overnight. If smells persist, change vinegar and repeat procedure nightly.

BEFORE

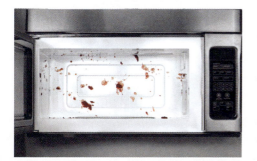

AFTER

Coffee and Teapots

- Buildup in a coffeemaker's brewing system can affect coffee flavor. Get rid of buildup by running a brewing cycle with cold water and 1/4 cup vinegar. Follow with a cycle of clean water. If you can still smell vinegar, run another cycle using fresh water.

- Remove coffee stains and mineral buildup from the glass pot of an automatic drip coffeemaker by adding 1 cup crushed ice, 1 tablespoon water, and 4 teaspoons salt to the pot when it is at room temperature. Gently swirl mixture, rinse, and wash as usual.

- To clean a teapot or stovetop percolator, fill it with water, add 2 or 3 tablespoons baking soda, and boil for 10 to 15 minutes. After cooling, scrub and rinse thoroughly.

- To clean the inside of a teapot, add the peel of 1 lemon per 2 cups warm water. Soak overnight.

Dishwasher

• Baking soda cleans your dishwasher inside and out. Dip a damp cloth in soda and use it to clean smudges and fingerprints from the exterior; the same method will also remove stains from the liner. Use a synthetic scouring pad to clean stubborn soil.

• Use a spray glass cleaner to polish chrome trim. Commercial kitchen-appliance waxes will leave a protective wax coating on your dishwasher, but be careful not to get wax on the plastic parts.

• Remove dried-on food or detergent from the chrome inside your dishwasher by rubbing with a piece of lemon. Wipe clean with a damp cloth, then rub dry with a clean, dry cloth.

• Add 1/2 cup vinegar to an empty dishwasher and run the rinse cycle. This will clear any clogs in the dishwasher drain lines and deodorize the machine.

Do you love your dishwasher? Thank Josephine Garis Cochran of Shelbyville, Illinois. In 1886, unable to find a machine to wash dishes more efficiently than her servants, she invented one. She received patent #355,139 for the first practical dish-washing machine. In 1893, she introduced her dishwasher at the Chicago World's Fair.

Containers

• When you finish a product that comes in a plastic squeeze bottle, don't toss the bottle in the recycling bin. Rinse it well and let it air-dry. These bottles are just right for storage of liquid solutions.

• Clean mineral deposits and neutralize any acids in old canning jars by shaking a solution of 4 tablespoons baking soda per quart of warm water inside. Rinse thoroughly, then sterilize as usual.

• Plasticware, especially food containers, often takes on a greasy feeling. Put a capful of bleach in the dishwater along with your usual dishwashing liquid. Problem solved!

• Scrub stained plastic storage containers with a paste of lemon juice and baking soda.

• Avoid red tomato stains on plastic by spraying a container with cooking spray before adding tomato-based food. Before washing the container, rinse with cold water.

Dinnerware and Glassware

Almost every meal you eat at home results in dirty dishes. That could be more than a thousand sinkfuls of dishes annually. Washing dishes is one of the few housecleaning tasks that is truly unavoidable; the trick is to get it done and out of the way as quickly as possible. Here are a few hints to help you do dishes without doing yourself in.

- Of course, the best hint for making dishwashing easier is to use a dishwasher. If you have a dishwasher, carefully read the manufacturer's instructions for loading, correct water temperatures, and preferred dishwasher detergents.

- Remove food residues from dinnerware as quickly as possible. Scrape dishes with a plastic brush to prevent scratches. Never scrape plates with knives or other sharp objects.

32 • Dinnerware and Glassware

• High temperatures may also damage dishes. Do not warm plates in the oven unless they are heatproof. Do not rinse glazed dinnerware with very hot or boiling water; this may cause the glaze to craze, or develop minute cracks.

• After the dishes are washed and you're ready to store them, insert a flattened coffee filter between china plates and saucers—or other delicate pieces—to protect them.

• Most glassware can be safely washed in the dishwasher, but gilt- and silver-trimmed glass, delicate crystal, milk glass, and ornamental glass must be washed by hand. If you have hard water in your area, we recommend that you wash all glassware by hand because the combination of hard water and dishwasher detergent will etch and permanently dull glassware.

Dinnerware and Glassware • 33

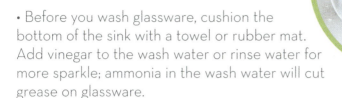

• Before you wash glassware, cushion the bottom of the sink with a towel or rubber mat. Add vinegar to the wash water or rinse water for more sparkle; ammonia in the wash water will cut grease on glassware.

• Wash glasses first, before cutlery or dinnerware. Slowly slide stemware into the wash water, holding the glass by the base; if you push a glass into the water bottom first, it could crack. Remove dirt from crevices with a soft-bristled brush; remove stains by rubbing with a cut lemon or washing in a vinegar solution. Let glassware drip dry upside down, or polish with a soft, lint-free cloth.

• Clean stained decanters by filling them with water and adding 1 cup ammonia or vinegar. Soak overnight. If this solution does not clean the decanter, use two packs of powdered denture cleaner dissolved in water.

• Crystal is best washed by hand, very carefully. After washing, dip crystal in a sink full of warm water and 1 tablespoon vinegar. Finish with a clear water rinse.

• Get rid of the cloudy film on glassware by soaking items overnight in a tub of equal parts vinegar and warm water. Wash glasses by hand the next day.

Flatware and Cutlery

Most of us wash the knives, forks, and spoons we use at mealtimes along with our other dishes. If we're organized and wash dishes by hand, the flatware is washed after the glasses and before the plates. But washing flatware doesn't complete the cleaning process; unless you eat with stainless steel, your flatware will need to be polished occasionally.

Cutlery (knives and other cutting instruments) can be cleaned in the same way as flatware, but observe the manufacturer's instructions to be sure that the cutlery is dishwasher safe. Here are some of the best methods we've found for cleaning and polishing flatware and cutlery.

- Always wash pewter and gold-plated flatware by hand and buff dry to bring up the shine and prevent water spots.

- Sterling silver and silver plate may be washed in the dishwasher, but they will need to be polished less often if they are washed by hand. Rinse salt and acid food off flatware as soon as possible to avoid stains.

- Do not soak flatware or cutlery that has bone, ivory, or wood handles; and do not wash them in the dishwasher.

- Use silver often; it tarnishes less and grows more beautiful with use. Store silver and gold flatware in rolls, bags, or cases made with tarnish-resistant cloth.

- If you need clean silver now instead of tomorrow morning, pour lemon juice over the piece. Polish with a soft, clean cotton cloth.

Flatware and Cutlery • 35

• Wash flatware and cutlery with liquid dishwashing detergent. Fill the sink with hot water, add the detergent, and wash the flatware using a soft cloth or sponge to wipe away the soil. Never use an abrasive cleanser, steel-wool pad, or synthetic scouring pad. Avoid overcrowding the sink to prevent scratching your flatware. After it is clean, rinse with hot water, and buff with a soft towel to bring up the shine.

• Give silverware a quick polish: Sprinkle some baking soda on a damp cloth or a sponge. Rub, rinse, and let dry.

• Shine up your silverware with a banana peel. Remove any leftover "strings" from the inside of the peel, then rub the peel on cutlery and serving pieces. Buff with a clean, soft cloth or a paper towel.

• Make a paste of cornstarch and water and apply to tarnished silverware. Let dry; wipe clean with a dry cloth.

Pots and Pans: Basic Care

When was the last time you saw your face reflected in the bottom of a skillet or reveled in the warm glow of a copper pot you had just shined? If you can't remember, you probably have much too much to do to worry about keeping your pots, pans, and cooking utensils looking like new. Unless they're on display, a reasonably clean cooking pot functions just about as well as a sparkling clean one does. The amount of shine on your cookware is totally up to you.

Basic care for all cookware starts with reading the manufacturer's care instructions. Wash all pots and pans thoroughly inside and out soon after use. An exception to this is your omelet pan. Clean seasoned omelet pans with a paper towel. If baked-on food necessitates washing the pan in soapsuds, dry it thoroughly over a warm burner and rub vegetable oil into the warm pan with a pad of folded paper toweling.

Prevent heat stains on the outsides of pans by keeping gas flames low so that they cannot lick up the sides. Do not subject cookware to sudden temperature changes. Allow it to cool before washing or soaking.

Clean scorched pans by bringing 1 teaspoon baking soda and 1 cup water to boil in the pan. Allow the pan to cool and wash it in soapy water. Substitute vinegar for baking soda to clean scorched aluminum pans.

Burned-on Food and Grease

- To loosen baked- or dried-on food in a pan, gently boil water and baking soda in the pan. When food is loosened, allow pan to cool and then wipe clean.

- Don't struggle to scrape off burned-on food in a pan. Pour in a can of cola; allow pan to soak for about an hour, then wipe clean.

- Use a steel-wool soap pad to remove burned-on food from cast-aluminum cookware. Liquid nonabrasive bathroom cleanser or a paste of baking soda and water used with a synthetic scouring pad will polish both cast and sheet aluminum.

- Get rid of excess grease in a roasting pan by sprinkling it with salt and wiping with a damp sponge or paper towel. Wash as usual.

- Reduce the chore of washing a greasy baking dish or pan. After the grease is drained off, rub the pan with a thick slice of lemon or a used lemon half turned inside out. Wash as usual.

Prevent and Remove Rust

• To remove rust from knives, cast-iron pots, and other kitchen equipment, make a paste with 1 part lemon juice and 2 parts salt. Apply with a clean, soft cloth and rub away the rust. Rinse with clear water; dry well.

• Get rid of rust on a kitchen knife by cutting an onion. Using the rusted blade, carefully cut into (but not all the way through) a large, whole onion. Repeat 2 or 3 times. If there is a large amount of rust on the blade, it may require a few more strokes to clean it off.

Stains and Discoloration

• To make stains vanish from aluminum or enamel cookware, fill the pot or pan with water and add a cut lime. Boil until the stains are gone. For a small pot, use half a lime; for a larger one, use both halves.

• The only way to protect aluminum cookware from discoloration is never to wash it in an automatic dishwasher or let it soak in soapy water for long periods of time. We recommend that you don't allow food to stand in aluminum cookware and don't use it to store food; food that is acid-based can discolor or pit the metal.

Cast-Iron Care ·············

- Cast-iron cookware has a tendency to rust if it is not kept properly seasoned. Some new cast-iron cooking utensils come from the factory already sealed, but most will have to be seasoned before their first use.

- Season cast-iron cookware in the traditional way: Scour your pot with a steel-wool soap pad, then wipe the inside with vegetable oil, place it in a warm oven for two hours, and wipe off the excess oil. To maintain your cookware's seasoning, repeat this procedure periodically and whenever rust spots appear.

- After seasoning a cast-iron skillet with a drop of vegetable oil, store it between 2 coffee filters to help keep moisture at bay.

- Wash cast-iron cookware in hot, sudsy water, then dry it thoroughly and store it in a dry cupboard without its lid in place. Never wash cast-iron cookware in the dishwasher; it will remove the seasoning and cause rust.

Copper Care

- Copper darkens with use and exposure to air. If you prefer shiny copper, you can clean and polish it easily. Copper cookware is lined with other metals to prevent harmful chemical reactions with food. The lining is usually tin or stainless steel. If your copper pot has a tin lining, you must be careful not to scrape away the tin by stirring with sharp metal cooking utensils. You can have a copper pan retinned when the lining begins to wear thin, but this is an expensive procedure. Use wood, nylon, or nonstick-coated spoons for stirring to prevent scratching the lining of copper cookware.

- Some copper cookware comes with a protective lacquer coating that must be removed before the utensil is heated. Follow the manufacturer's instructions, or place the utensil in a solution of 1 cup baking soda and 2 gallons boiling water, let it stand until the water is cool, peel off the lacquer, wash, rinse, and dry.

- Protect copper pans from scorching by making sure there is always liquid or fat in the pan before it is placed on the heat. When melting butter, swirl it around in the bottom of the pan and up the sides. Lower the heat as soon as the contents of the pot reach the boiling point.

- Commercial copper-cleaning products do a good job of cleaning and shining copper cookware if you follow the manufacturer's instructions.

Non-Stick Cookware

• Non-stick finishes or coatings are relatively thin and damage easily. We recommend that you use wood, nylon, or specially coated spoons and spatulas to prevent surface damage. Most nonstick-coated cookware can be safely washed in the dishwasher.

• Wash new non-stick pans before using them and lightly coat the inside with vegetable oil. Apply vegetable oil again after each washing in the dishwasher and after treating stains. Do not soak pans in soapy water; the coating can retain a soap flavor.

Small Appliances

• To clean the cutting wheel of your can opener, "open" a paper towel or two. Close the cutting wheel on the edge of the paper towel, grip the handles together, and turn the crank. The towel will wipe off crud as the wheel cuts it.

• A cotton swab can be used to clean the hard-to-reach places on your kitchen blender, electric mixer, or electric can opener. Dip the swab in warm, soapy water, then scrub and rinse.

• To clean a pancake griddle, pour brewed coffee onto the surface (which can be warm or cold). Wait a few minutes, then wipe clean with a soft cloth, making sure the surface has cooled before you do this.

IN THE BATHROOM

Ironically, the smallest room in the house is the one that demands to be cleaned most frequently. In this section, we'll provide some tips to help you out.

Daily Cleaning Tips

In the bathroom, more is less! If you and everyone who uses the bathroom quick-cleans it every day, you'll ultimately spend less time cleaning it. Fortunately, most bathrooms are made of materials that are easy to keep clean. Tile and porcelain surfaces are stain-resistant if dirt and scum are not allowed to build up on them.

Daily Cleaning Tips • 47

• Make it a firm rule in your home to rinse out the tub or shower stall immediately after you use it. Rinse it while you are still wet and in the tub or stall. Simply spray water from the shower head on all interior surfaces, then lather soap onto a damp sponge, swish it around the tub or stall, and rinse.

• Some shower sprays don't even need rinsing—just spray and walk away!

• The basin can be given a similar treatment each evening by the last person who uses it.

• Keeping tile and porcelain surfaces clean so that they never need to be scoured not only saves time, but it also protects these surfaces from unnecessary wear and keeps them looking their best.

* To keep the bathtub and tiles free of soap scum, rinse thoroughly after each use, and rub the surfaces with a cut lemon. The same method—rubbing surfaces with a cut lemon—can remove many sink and tub rust stains.

* Undiluted bleach in a spray bottle tackles serious bathroom grime. Spray the tub, sink, ceramic tile, or shower surfaces, wait a few minutes, and wipe clean with a damp sponge.

Countertops

Bathroom countertops are sloshed, splotched, and splattered with everything from hair spray to shoe polish. In most homes, countertops are made of materials that can stand up to the assault: ceramic tile, cultured marble, and plastic laminate. Because these materials are durable, they are easy to clean.

Cultured marble resembles real marble, but it is a lot more versatile and much easier to care for. Unlike plastic laminate, cultured marble is not a thin veneer; if you scratch or burn it, you can often repair the damage.

Avoid using abrasive cleaners and steel-wool pads to clean cultured marble; they will scratch the surface, making it difficult to keep clean. Mildly abrasive liquid and powdered cleansers should be applied directly to the wet surface of the countertop to dissolve dirt and soap film. Rinse well, and buff dry with a soft cloth.

Plastic laminate is very durable if you don't scratch it, chip it, knock off its edges, burn it, scrub it, let water seep under it, stain it, or otherwise mistreat it. Plastic laminate is made of thin layers of plastic superimposed on craft paper and overlaid on particle board or plywood. The color of most plastic laminate is only in the top layer. The glossy, matte, or textured surface is also laid on. This is the reason plastic laminate cannot be restored if it is damaged; all its beauty is on the surface.

Regularly apply an appliance wax or light furniture wax to protect and brighten plastic-laminate surfaces.

During your bathroom-cleaning session, wipe your plastic-laminate countertop with a damp cloth or sponge. A two-sided scrubbing pad with fiber on one side and a sponge on the other works especially well. Moistened slightly with water, the fiber side is just abrasive enough to loosen greasy smears and other soil. Turning the scrubber over, use the sponge side to wipe the surface damp-dry.

When a spot or stain persists, first sprinkle baking soda on the spot and scrub gently. If this doesn't take care of the problem, apply a polishing cleanser with a wet sponge.

Ancient Cleaning Secrets

Around 600 B.C., the Phoenicians made soap from goat's tallow (fat) and wood ashes; they sometimes used it as an article of barter with the Gauls.

The Celts used animal fats and plant ashes and named the product *saipo*, from which the English word soap is derived.

Beginning in the second century A.D., at the suggestion of the Greek physician Galen, soap was used for washing and cleaning (instead of as a medicine).

Showers and Bathtubs

• To clean gunky shower tracks, use a shower track and grout brush. If you don't have one, wrap very fine steel wool around an old toothbrush and scrub the tracks. Spray glass cleaner all over the tracks; wipe clean.

• Loosen up soap scum on shower doors and walls with an all-purpose bathroom cleaner or by spraying them with vinegar. Let dry, then respray to dampen. Wipe clean. Reapply and let sit for several hours. Then dampen and wipe clean again.

• Shower curtains can become dulled by soap film or plagued with mildew. Keep vinegar in a spray bottle near your shower, and squirt shower curtains once or twice a week. No need to rinse.

• Fight mildew stains and lightly clean a shower curtain by sprinkling baking soda on a sponge and scrubbing. Rinse well.

• To remove mineral and mildew stains from a shower curtain, first soak it in salt water for 15 to 20 minutes. Hang to drain excess water. Rub the stains with lemon juice while the curtain is still damp. Wipe with a damp sponge, rinse with clean water, or run through the washing machine.

Showers and Bathtubs

- Prevent mildew growth on a shower curtain by soaking it in a bathtub full of salt water (1/2 cup salt to the tub). Soak for several hours, then hang to dry.

- Those sunflower decals may have looked cute when you stuck them on the tub to prevent slips and falls, but now they're chipped, stained, and probably out of fashion. To get rid of them, loosen the glue by saturating each decal with vinegar. (Warm vinegar in microwave for about 3 minutes for better results.) Let vinegar sit for a few minutes, then peel off decals. You should be able to remove any leftover glue by scrubbing with a damp sponge.

- Stains on nonskid strips or appliques in the tub can be removed by first dampening the area, then sprinkling with baking soda. Let sit for 20 minutes; scrub and rinse.

- If your bathroom never seems to be fully dry and you are going away for some time, place a large, shallow box of nonclumping cat litter in your bathtub to absorb moisture.

Sinks ························

• Attack stubborn rust stains in a sink (or tub) with a paste of cream of tartar and hydrogen peroxide. Apply the paste, then scrub clean with a nonabrasive pad or brush. Rinse completely.

• Plug the drain in your bathroom sink, pour in 1/2 cup vinegar, then fill the sink with water. Let sit 1 hour, then scrub any mineral deposit areas with an old toothbrush. Rinse.

• Pour isopropyl rubbing alcohol on a paper towel to remove smudges and hairspray from chrome faucets.

• Clean chrome with club soda. Pour some on a clean, soft cloth and dab it on. Buff to a shine with a second cloth.

BEFORE   **AFTER**

Mildew Fighters

• When mildew is multiplying in out-of-the-way spots, place a few cotton balls soaked in bleach in the area. Wait a few hours, then wipe clean with a sponge dampened with warm water.

• Use a mildew stain remover, or mix equal amounts of vinegar and water in a spray bottle. Spray onto mildewed areas and let sit for 15 minutes. Wipe clean.

• Undiluted isopropyl rubbing alcohol can remove small areas of mildew buildup on grout, caulk, or tile. Dip a cloth into the alcohol and scrub.

• Mildew may make a habit of building up on your shower and tub accessories. Mix 1 1/2 cups bleach with 2 gallons water and scrub bath mats, curtains, and soap dishes with the mixture, using a sponge or a scrub brush. Rinse.

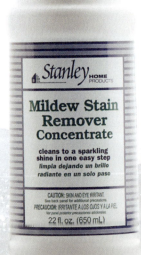

Grout

- A 9" brush is a great tool for cleaning dirty grout in hard to reach places.

- For tough grout or tile stains, use a paste of 1 part bleach to 3 parts baking soda.

- Use a paste of baking soda and water to remove mildew stains on grout. Apply, scrub with an old toothbrush, and rinse.

- For everyday cleaning of tile and grout, rub with a little apple cider vinegar on a sponge. This gives off a pleasant scent and will help cut any greasy buildup.

Smell-Busters

- Sprinkle baking soda in the bathroom trash can after each emptying.

- A dryer sheet can control odor and musty smells under your bathroom sink.

- Add a perpetual air freshener to the toilet area by keeping baking soda in a pretty dish on top of the tank. Add your favorite scented bath salts to the mix if desired. Change every 3 months.

- When you hang a new roll of toilet paper, loosely roll up a dryer sheet and place it inside the paper core. The fresh scent will disperse through the small room.

Toilets

Cleaning the toilet is one of those grin-and-bear-it chores that you want to get through as quickly as possible. Many toilet-bowl cleaners and deodorizers claim that they'll help you do this. Some products are truly helpful, some are not. Some cleaners are placed in the tank and dispense solution each time the toilet is flushed. Even the best in-tank cleaner, though, is not a substitute for a regular scrubbing, when you also clean the seat and the rim of the toilet bowl.

Toilet bowls and tanks usually are made of vitreous china, which is nonporous and easy to clean. Before you clean your toilet, read the label on your cleaning product to learn its exact chemical makeup and how it should be used. Be especially careful never to mix products that contain chlorine bleach with ammonia-based products. Always wear rubber gloves when you work with toilet cleaners. They contain strong chemicals and should be flushed immediately after the bowl has been cleaned. Unless directed otherwise, you should be careful not to allow chemical cleaners to remain in the toilet or to touch other bathroom surfaces.

We suggest that you keep a long-handled brush for cleaning only toilet bowls.

The exterior of a toilet should be cleaned with the same products you use for tubs and basins. Wipe the toilet seat, the tank, around the rim, and around the base when you clean.

- Once a week, pour 2 cups vinegar into toilet and let it sit. (Tip: Rest toilet bowl brush inside bowl with lid closed to remind yourself and family members not to use the toilet until it gets brushed!) After 8 hours or more, brush toilet well; flush. This regular treatment will keep hard-water stains at bay and clean and freshen your bowl between major cleanings.

- A half cup of baking soda in the toilet bowl will work for light cleaning. Let sit for 30 minutes, then brush and flush.

- To remove toilet bowl stains, pour in a can of cola. Wait 1 hour, then brush bowl clean and flush.

- Clean your toilet by putting 2 denture cleanser tablets in the bowl and letting them sit overnight. Then scrub the toilet in the morning.

- Clean your toilet while you're not even home! Pour 1/4 cup bleach into the bowl, but don't flush the toilet until you return—even days later. (Be sure to close the bathroom door before you leave if pets will be around.)

Indoor plumbing was becoming a "fixture" by about 1870, replacing chamber pots, buckets, and portable washing basins. As early as 1778, Joseph Bramah of London invented the metal valve-type water closet. Other early sinks, toilets, and bathtubs also were made of metal—primarily lead, copper, and zinc. They were hard to clean, however, so in the mid-1870s Thomas Twyford made a ceramic toilet and wash-down water closet. Because ceramics are too brittle for bathtubs, the porcelain-enamel cast-iron tub was invented. The double-shell, built-in style still common today was introduced around 1915.

Drains

In most homes, the bathroom sink is a dressing table as well as a washbasin, and everyone in the family shampoos in the shower. Hair and soap are washed into bathroom drains day and night, and the cruddy mess can quickly jam up the works. All that is needed to clean some clogged drains is to clear the trap of hair and soap curds. Regular clearing of the traps saves your plumbing, and It also cuts down on cleaning time, since when water flows out of the basin and tub quickly, it doesn't allow dirt to settle on these surfaces.

When clearing the trap doesn't clear the drain, you'll have to take stronger measures. First, use a plumber's helper and plunge the drain. (We suggest that you keep one handy in the bathroom.) Before you use the plunger in the bathroom basin, plug the overflow opening. This allows the plunger to exercise its maximum suction effect on the clogged drain.

If plunging does not open the drain, use a chemical drain opener. These products must be handled with special care because they are caustic and harmful to skin and eyes. Use them in a well-ventilated area, and follow the manufacturer's instructions. Commercial drain openers are sold in granular, liquid, and pressurized forms. Granular products utilize lye to do their work, liquid drain openers use lye and other

chemicals, and pressurized products work by chlorofluorocarbon propellants and pressure. If you use a granular drain opener, you must first remove standing water from the sink; this is not necessary for liquid and pressurized products.

Chemical drain openers will damage porcelain enamel and should not be allowed to remain on the surface of your fixtures for any length of time.

If the first type of chemical drain opener you use does not work, do not use a different chemical drain cleaner unless the initial cleaner has been flushed away totally. Never use a plunger or a pressurized drain opener after using a chemical cleaner; it may cause dangerous chemicals to splash back onto you. Also, be sure to tell your plumber what you have put into the drain before he or she starts to work. The combination of ammonia and other household cleaners with chemical drain openers produces hazardous gases.

Mirrors

The better your family's dental hygiene, the sooner you'll see spots before your eyes when you look in the bathroom mirror. As is true of other bathroom surfaces, daily wiping both delays and facilitates heavy-duty cleaning. You can quickly remove spots and spatters from a mirror with a damp facial tissue, and then polish it with a dry one.

• If your mirror is clouded by hair spray, rubbing alcohol will wipe away the haze.

• During the morning rush hour, if you're trying to shave while the shower is producing billows of steam in the same small bathroom, you can defog the bathroom mirror quickly by blowing hot air on it with a hair dryer. Running an inch of cold water in the bathtub before adding hot water eliminates fogging altogether.

• Pour vinegar into a shallow bowl or pan, then crumple a sheet of newspaper, dip it in the vinegar, and apply to the mirror. Wipe the glass several times with the same newspaper until the mirror is almost dry, then shine it with a clean, soft cloth or dry newspaper.

Solving Bathroom Clutter

• The obvious solution to bathroom clutter is to create storage for the things most bathrooms are not designed to store, such as hair dryers, makeup, electric shavers, and magazines. Clear countertops not only look cleaner, but they are quicker to clean, because there's no clutter to clean around and under.

• Bring some order to that bathroom or bedroom drawer. A plastic ice cube tray is the perfect organizer for small items such as bobby pins, hair clips, safety pins, earrings, rings, and spare change.

• So that you won't misplace frequently used items, glue small magnets on the walls of the medicine cabinet to hold nail files, cuticle scissors, clippers, and other small metal objects.

• Your medicine cabinet will stay neat and clean with shelf paper made of blotters that can absorb medicine or cosmetic spills.

A Few Last Tips

• Wish you could turn those slippery slivers of soap into something other than trash? Collect them in a sandwich-size food storage bag. When the bag is about half full, place it in a pot of warm—but not boiling—water. Remove when the soap melts. When it cools, you'll have a new bar of soap.

• Alternately, whenever a bar becomes too small to handle, cut slits in a sponge and tuck in the soap pieces. Or, put the slivers in a clean child-size sock to make a soaped up washcloth. Both are perfect for your child's bath time.

• A large binder clip placed on the end of a tube of toothpaste or similar packaging will ensure that you'll get all your money's worth.

• Soak toothbrushes overnight in a solution of 4 tablespoons baking soda to 1 quart warm water.

• Soak dentures, athletic mouthguards, retainers, or other oral appliances in a solution of 2 teaspoons baking soda dissolved in a glass of warm water. Another option is to scrub these items using an old toothbrush dipped in baking soda.